Little kitty in the big city

dedication - to the cats we love
Binky   Tab   Othello   Dinah

Little Kitty
Happy as could be
Perched on the porch
Thinks he's carefree

But as Little Kitty
Sits at home
Something is missing
Feeling alone

Longing to leave
Kitty loves his home
But Kitty is restless
He wants to roam

He has an idea
And is getting giddy
Kitty will move
to New York City

Packs his things
Ready to go
Little Kitty
Is in the flow

All aboard!
The conductor says
Start the engine
Full steam ahead!

Walks down the aisle
Finds his seat
Excited for the journey
Kicks back his feet

Looks out the window
Far out in the sky
The buildings in the distance
Catch his eye

8

The train screeches
And begins to slow
Kitty's excitement
Is starting to grow

Jumps out of his seat
Ready to explore
Kitty grabs his bags
Walks out the door

10

On the prowl
Walking down the street
Excited to find out
Who he'll meet

Walking around
Kitty comes to a stop
Finds his new home
Above a shop

Kitty looks around
Likes what he sees
Reaches to his pocket
And grabs the keys

Walks up to the door
And gives it a knock
Turns the key
And opens the lock

Little Kitty drops his bag on the ground
Stops for a moment to have a look around

The rooms are small
The doors squeak
But Kitty's apartment
Is very chic

16

Sleepy from the ride
His little legs
Are feeling fried

Sits upon the windowsill
Trying to relax
With some time to kill

He dozes off
But, wakes in a fright
The feeling of falling
Like he's taking flight

Falls out the window
And onto the street
Luckily, he landed
On his feet

A Fireman rushes
Over to see
If Little Kitty
Landed pain free

The Fireman says
Don't worry Little Kitty
There is nothing to fear
In the big city!

Now Little Kitty
Walks down the street
Feeling hungry
Needs something to eat

Looks for a snack
Can't find any mice
So Little Kitty
Buys a slice

Walks to the park
Ready to eat
Finds a bench
To rest his feet

Picks up his head
To look at the lights
Little Kitty
Takes in the sights

In the distance
Kitty can see
A bird swooping down
From a tree

Pigeon looks tired after his flight
So Little Kitty gives him a bite

Pigeon looks like someone to trust
So Little Kitty shares his crust

Little Kitty
Happy as could be
Made a new friend
In the Big city

Playing in the park
Trees whizzing by
Having a ball
Time is starting to fly

30

Kitty and Pigeon
Leaving the park
Ready for more
But it's getting dark

Kitty walks home
Pigeon comes for the ride
Kitty's new friend
Is by his side

Pigeon says to Kitty
tomorrow he'll be back
And this time
he'll bring the snack

Pigeon waves goodbye
As he fly's away

34

Kitty is thrilled
He made a friend today

Kitty climbs up the stairs
And opens the door

Sees his bed
On the floor

Wants to be cozy
Needs some heat
Kitty curls up
At his owners' feet

Closes his eyes
Comfy in bed
Excited for the adventures
That lay ahead

While falling asleep Kitty cracks a smile
He could get used to the big city for a while

The End

What happens when twins and the best of friends find out that they are more different than they are alike? Follow Veggie and Angus as they discover that going down different paths can also lead them back together again. This charming story, set in the small town of Foodsville, encourages children to enthusiastically follow their interests, while never forgetting the importance of always being there for family.

"I thought he was joking when he told me he was going to write a children's book about cheeseburgers"
-Robert's Brother Joe

What happens when Mr. Kitty and Jack are snowed in for the day? This heartwarming story shows how cooking can strengthen the bond between a father and son.

"He had too much fun writing the cat puns, it was concerning"
-Robert's Dad

"I wish he could just say he was proud of me"
-Robert about his Dad's quote

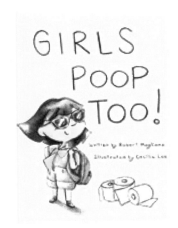

There comes a point in every girl's life when they have to poop. Unfortunately, girls of all ages often feel embarrassed when they have to perform a normal bodily function. Our book is intended to bring humor to a traditionally taboo subject in hope of creating a normalcy around the topic of girls performing a number two.

"Rob is really silly"
-Robert's Nieces Bianca & Avelina

About the Author:

Robert Magliano is a children's book author born and raised in New York. Robert works in innovation and strategy at a luxury retail company in New York City by day and is a children's book author by night. His debut book The Adventures of Veggie & Angus Burger encouraged children to embrace their differences and to always be there for one another. In his second book, Mr. Kitty's Kitchen, Robert hoped to teach children to develop positive relationships with their friends and family through cooking. Robert's third book Girls Poop Too, was inspired by his nieces being embarrassed to go number two at a young age. When Robert and his nieces searched for a book to address this issue, they couldn't find one so, they asked him to write one specifically for them. Robert is passionate about family, friends, and food. He is excited to continue writing and exploring new concepts.

Robert was recently married the love of his life, Annie, who has the honor and privilege of listening to him talk about cheeseburgers and cat puns all day.

42

Gwendolyn Tetirick's love for her childhood cat and her dream of bringing Othello to New York City inspired the writing of Little Kitty in the Big City. Gwendolyn is a painter who appreciates the art of illustration to bring this whimsical story to life. Gwendolyn works in luxury fashion in New York City and pursues her passions of creativity, community, and animals. She looks forward to future books intended to teach children about exploring new places and forming new friendships.

CPSIA information can be obtained
at www.ICGtesting.com
Printed in the USA
BVHW060929071221
623416BV00009B/1484